CONFUCIUS

CHINESE PHILOSOPHER AND TEACHER

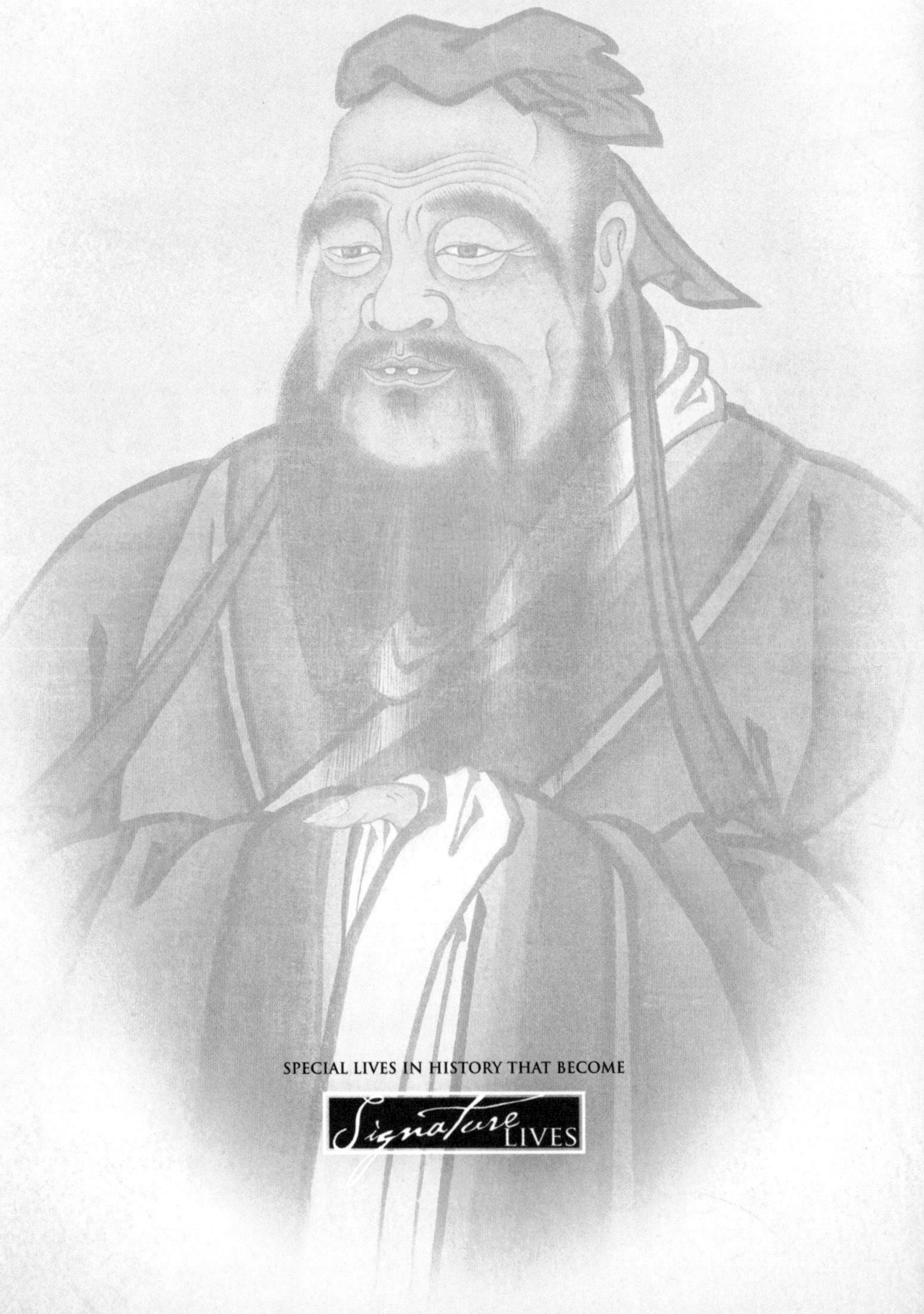

SPECIAL LIVES IN HISTORY THAT BECOME

Signature LIVES

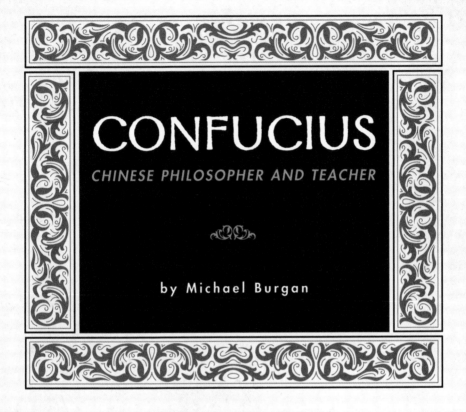

CONFUCIUS
CHINESE PHILOSOPHER AND TEACHER

by Michael Burgan

Content Adviser: Carol Stepanchuk,
Outreach Coordinator, Center for Chinese Studies,
University of Michigan

Reading Adviser: Rosemary G. Palmer, Ph.D.,
Department of Literacy, College of Education,
Boise State University

Compass Point Books ✦ Minneapolis, Minnesota

Compass Point Books
151 Good Counsel Drive
P.O. Box 669
Mankato, MN 56002-0669

Editor: Julie Gassman
Page Production: Bobbie Nuytten
Photo Researcher: Svetlana Zhurkin
Cartographer: XNR Productions, Inc.
Library Consultant: Kathleen Baxter

Art Director: LuAnn Ascheman-Adams
Creative Director: Keith Griffin
Editorial Director: Nick Healy
Managing Editor: Catherine Neitge

Library of Congress Cataloging-in-Publication Data
Burgan, Michael.
    Confucius: Chinese philosopher and teacher / by Michael Burgan.
        p. cm. — (Signature lives)
    Includes bibliographical references and index.
    ISBN 978-0-7565-3832-3 (library binding)
    1. Confucius–Juvenile literature. 2. Philosophers—China—Biography—
Juvenile literature. I. Title. II. Series.
    B128.C8B 87 2008
    181'.112—dc22
    [B]   2008006283

Visit Compass Point Books on the Internet at *www.compasspointbooks.com*
or e-mail your request to *custserv@compasspointbooks.com*

ANCIENT WORLD

Societies of long ago were peopled with unique men and women who would make their mark on the world. As we learn more and more about them, we continue to marvel at their accomplishments. We enjoy their works of art and literature. And we acknowledge that their beliefs, their actions, and their lives led to the world we know today. These men and women would make—and change—history.

Confucius

Table of Contents

In this book, the romanization of Chinese words—changing
Chinese characters to letters of the Roman alphabet—follows the
pinyin system, the official system of the People's Republic of China.

至聖孔子

兗州府曲阜縣人

1 RULING THE RIGHT WAY

⊸⟨✕⟩⊷

For years, the great scholar Confucius had a single goal: to serve as a top adviser to one of the rulers of China. At the time, around 500 B.C., China was divided into many kingdoms. Within the kingdoms, dukes and princes controlled vast stretches of land. Confucius ached to hold an important government position. Then he could use his knowledge to improve how leaders ruled, which would better the lives of common people.

Many of Confucius' words and actions are recorded in the *Analects*, a book that was written by some of Confucius' students after his death. The students wanted to share their teacher's great wisdom with others and give him the respect they thought he deserved. The *Analects* report that Confucius, known

Confucius is considered one of the most influential figures of Chinese history.

as "the Master," once said:

> If there were any of the princes who would employ me, in the course of twelve months, I should have done something considerable. In three years, the government would be perfected.

Confucius was confident that his thoughts and actions could improve any country.

But several things kept Confucius from his goal. Most of the important government positions were held by nobles and their families. The jobs were passed from fathers to sons, even if the sons lacked the right skills. And few leaders in China were eager to hire a man like Confucius. He closely followed the moral teachings of China's greatest books. He expected others around him to follow the same strict sense of right and wrong. And he would not hesitate to tell people—even dukes or princes—when they had

The man much of the world knows today as Confucius was never called that during his lifetime. As a boy, his first name was Qiu, and his family name was Kong (also spelled K'ung). He also had the name Zhongni, which he received when he became an adult. The students who studied and sometimes traveled with Confucius called him Kong Fuzi or Kongzi, which means "Master Kong." In the 17th century, Roman Catholic priests called Jesuits came to China to spread their religion. They learned Chinese and began translating the works of Master Kong into Latin, the language used by Catholic scholars of that time. These translators created the name Confucius out of Kong Fuzi.

strayed from the ancient teachings. The leaders wanted advisers who followed orders and told them how wonderful they were. Few of them were eager to hear Confucius' honest and challenging words.

Eventually, Confucius was given a government job in his homeland of Lu. Historians are not sure what job Confucius held, but he was certainly on the lowest level of government officials. In the past, Confucius had taught that talented men should not take a job in government if they could not do great things. But Mencius, a later scholar who followed many of

Mencius traveled to various states to convince rulers to follow Confucius' way.

Confucius' teachings, said Confucius still hoped he could play a key role in government. Mencius wrote that Confucius "took office ... because he saw that there was a possibility that his doctrines might be practiced."

Confucius hoped the leaders of Lu would ask for his advice on important issues, but they rarely did. Instead, he took part in ceremonies for guests when they came to Qufu, the capital of Lu. The *Analects* noted that one of his duties was to tell the duke of Lu when visitors had left the throne room. He also sometimes carried the duke's scepter, a rod that was a symbol of royal power.

Confucius seems to have advised some officials on a military matter. Three powerful families in Lu sometimes fought each other and the duke for control of the kingdom. Each family had built large forts that served as walled cities. At times, the governors of these cities rebelled, knowing they could easily defend their home forts. Confucius convinced the duke of Lu to tell the three families to take down the forts. This would help end the threat of rebellion and unify Lu. Two of the forts came down, but the last family resisted.

Around this time, the neighboring kingdom of Qi sent the duke of Lu a gift. Eighty beautiful women, skilled in singing and dancing, appeared in Qufu. The duke of Qi seemed to have opposed Confucius' plan to take down forts. The threat of rebellion from the three families kept the duke of Lu from building a strong government and central army. As long as Lu was divided, it was weakened and less of a threat to Qi. The rulers of Qi wanted to make sure Lu stayed weak. The dancing girls sent from Qi were supposed to distract Lu's leaders. One historian suggests that the presence of the women was meant to offend Confucius and his morals.

The Ji, one of the three powerful families of Lu, welcomed the women into the capital. For three days, no official business went on, as the leaders spent time with the young women. The *Analects* say that Confucius left Lu at this time. Perhaps he was offended. But most likely, he realized he could never truly reform the government as he had hoped.

Now in his mid-50s, Confucius began to wander across the kingdoms of China. He desperately sought a ruler who would

The teachings of Confucius led to a system of thought called Confucianism. To followers of this system, the second-greatest thinker after Confucius was Meng-tzu, or Mencius. He was born sometime around 372 or 371 B.C. and died around 289. His family came from Zou, a small state next to Confucius' homeland of Lu. Mencius learned the teachings of Confucius from a man who had studied with Confucius' grandson. Like Confucius, Mencius held various government jobs as he tried to teach China's leaders the best way to rule. His writings are collected in a book simply called the Mencius. *In it, he records some of the words supposedly spoken by Confucius.*

Some women in ancient China, such as those sent to Lu, were trained to entertain men with singing and dancing.

follow his advice. For 10 years he searched, but he had little success. The true influence of Confucius and his teachings would have to wait until hundreds of years after his death.

Scholars such as Mencius honored Confucius and his work. The Master's teachings and writings were studied carefully. Finally, during the second century B.C., Confucius' goal was realized; the ruling emperor of China used Confucian ideas to run his government.

Some people have called Confucianism a religion, because the Master and his followers believed Heaven influenced and inspired humans. And at times, Confucius himself was honored as a kind of god. But Confucianism is really a set of beliefs about the proper way for people to act, whether or not they believe in God or spirits.

Confucianism influenced China and neighboring countries for centuries. Even today, the influence of the Master is felt in Asia and wherever people have accepted his teachings on moral actions. Confucius has been compared to Greek philosophers, Christianity's Jesus Christ, and the Indian religious figure Buddha for providing rules for the right way to act.

For centuries after Confucius lived, many educated Chinese tried to follow his teachings and the ideas of other great Chinese thinkers of his era, such as Mencius. When the Jesuits arrived in China, they began putting all these ideas into a single system of thought, which they named for Confucius. Some historians argue today that with this process, the Jesuits created what is now called Confucianism. They say the Chinese never saw Confucius as the main figure in a formal system, as the Jesuits did. Scholars still debate the exact nature of Confucianism.

2 LEARNING AND SERVING

Nothing about Confucius' childhood hinted that he would one day influence half of Asia. By some accounts, he grew up an orphan. Others say he lived with his mother, who struggled to provide for her son after his father's death. Confucius himself said, "We were poor when I was young, so I learned many a menial [lowly] skill."

But the stories say that Confucius did have ties to a grand past. His father may have been Shuliang He, a skilled warrior who fought for a powerful family, the Meng. Shuliang's family had once belonged to the nobility, but it had lost its power and money through battles with rival families. Shuliang won his own honor with bravery on the battlefield. In one battle, he and his men helped a noble family escape

One legend about Confucius says that as a child, he pretended to act out religious ceremonies for play.

their palace, which was surrounded by enemies. Another source describes Shuliang and his men storming an enemy fort. The enemy had left the gate open, hoping to trap the invaders. Shuliang managed to hold open a closing gate so he and his men could escape the trap.

Some sources say Shuliang was in his 50s when he met Confucius' mother. Her name is not recorded in early accounts of Confucius' life, but some later books call her Zhengzai. Shuliang already had a wife and children, so he and Zhengzai might not have married. Though at this time, Chinese men did sometimes have more than one wife.

Legends written long after Confucius' death said that his mother dreamed about her son before he was born. In the dream, she saw spirits leading a unicorn, which meant her child would do great things. Confucius' disciples created such stories so people would think he was meant to be an important leader.

Zhengzai was living in the town of Zou when Confucius was born in 551 B.C. This town and all of what was Lu were located in the modern Chinese province of Shandong. Zhengzai nicknamed her son Qiu ("mound") because of a bump on his head.

When Confucius was 3, his father died. Living in poverty with his mother, he learned firsthand how hard life could be for the poor. Yet he also had ties through his father to the ruling class. Some

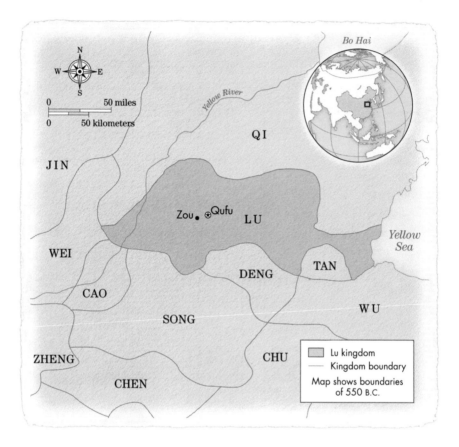

Map shows boundaries of 550 B.C.

historians think that the Meng family might have helped educate Confucius.

As a boy, Confucius probably learned his lessons by listening to adults, not reading books. Books were uncommon in China during the sixth century B.C. The "paper" was actually strips of bamboo tied together with pieces of leather. Only government officials and the richest families owned books. The writing system of China, then and now, used figures called

Zou, where Confucius was born, was less than 20 miles (32 kilometers) from Qufu, where he spent much of his life.

characters to record words. Each character is made up of a series of brush strokes, and most words have two or more characters.

Confucius' schooling probably also included learning music and singing songs. Later in life, he often spoke about the importance of music and mentioned songs written in the *Book of Songs*, an ancient Chinese collection of poetry and songs. As an adult, Confucius once told his students:

> *Reciting the Songs can ... strengthen your powers of observation, enhance your ability to get along with others, and sharpen your critical skills. Close at hand it enables you to serve your father, and away at court it enables you to serve your lord [ruler].*

Confucius believed the songs offered wisdom for the correct way to live.

According to the *Analects*, Confucius stated that "from 15 [years old], my heart-and-mind was set on learning." Most likely, he continued

The Chinese use tens of thousands of characters to write their language. The average educated Chinese regularly uses about 5,000 or 6,000 of them. To write Chinese words in English, the characters are translated using one of two systems. The first system is called Wade-Giles, named for two British scholars. In recent years, it has been replaced by a system called Hanyu Pinyin, or simply pinyin. This system was developed in China during the 1950s and became the official translation system in 1979. It is preferred because experts agree that pinyin produces a word that sounds more like the original Chinese.

his education while working for the government at low-level jobs in Qufu. Mencius records that Confucius ran a grain warehouse, and later he was in charge of raising farm animals. Confucius said about his jobs, "I keep accurate records ... I make sure the cattle and sheep grow strong."

Historians know few details about Confucius' life as a young adult. At 19, he married, and he eventually had two children—a son and a daughter—who reached adulthood. When the boy was born, the duke of Lu sent Confucius a carp as a present. The

The carp, often depicted on Chinese art, was a symbol of abundance and success.

duke would not have given gifts to all new fathers. The gift of the fish might have meant that the son was born after Confucius had already impressed others with his talents. Confucius named his new son Li—Chinese for "carp"—but the boy was later known by his nickname, Boyu. This meant "Top Fish." His sister, whose name is not known, later married one of Confucius' students, Kung-ye Chang. Some sources say Confucius had a second daughter who died young. Nothing has been recorded about Confucius' wife.

Confucius also helped take care of his older half-brother, who had some sort of physical problem. The brother, called Mengpi in one source, could not carry out his family duties. In China at that time, those duties included performing religious rites in the home and choosing a husband for a daughter. Mengpi had a daughter, and when she was old enough to marry, Confucius took on the duty of finding her a husband.

When Confucius was in his early 20s, his mother died. His government jobs had helped him build some wealth, and he spent time and money having his mother buried. He tracked down the site of his father's grave and then had the body removed so it could be buried again next to his mother. He had both graves dug in the town of Fang. Then Confucius followed the customs expected of Chinese children when their parents died. Since the parents had spent so much time and energy raising the child during his or her first two or three years, the child was supposed to mourn their deaths just as long. For three years, Confucius stayed home, mourning his mother and studying.

Later in life, talking about the importance of behaving correctly, he said, "I cannot bear to see …

It was customary to honor dead relatives with sacrificial offerings, such as food.

mourners who do not truly grieve." One of Confucius' students once suggested that one year was plenty to mourn a dead parent. The Master noted, "It is only after being tended by his parents for three years that an infant can finally leave their bosom [care]."

Following tradition and studying the past became increasingly important for Confucius. At the time, China was going through a period of political and social crisis. The various Chinese states fought each other, sometimes sending hundreds of chariots into battle. From these horse-drawn carts, soldiers fired arrows. Armies might include 100,000 soldiers clashing on an open field. The poor peasants of China often paid the price for the wars of the ruling nobles. During war, they were forced to leave their farms and serve as foot soldiers. If captured by the enemy, they could be forced into slavery. The different kingdoms also faced the threat of invasion from neighboring peoples. The Chinese referred to them as barbarians. Confucius thought that the actions and thoughts of ancient rulers offered clues for solving the

Ancient China's peasants were considered the lowest class, below nobles and officers. These positions were inherited, and one could not rise up to a higher status. Peasants were supposed to serve those above them, while the superiors were supposed to make sure the peasants were provided for. During times of war, however, peasants were heavily taxed to help pay for the war. If their crops were poor, there was no money to help them, and they were often left to starve.

current problems.

In his studies of past leaders, Confucius was especially influenced by the early rulers of the Zhou Dynasty. The Zhou Dynasty was founded by King Wen. Just before he died, Wen ordered his son Wu to

A fifth-century A.D. terra-cotta statue depicts a Chinese warrior on horseback.

attack the ruling Shang Dynasty. So in the 11th century B.C., the Zhou rebelled against the dynasty. The Shang leaders, it was said, drank too much alcohol and mistreated their people. After their rebellion, the Zhou claimed they had a religious right to get rid of the Shang. Since they had been successful in defeating the Shang, they must have had the approval of the Chinese god known as Tian, or "Heaven" in English. The Zhou kings said the mandate, or will, of Heaven gave them the right to rule.

Wu attacked his enemy on horseback, a successful war strategy in ancient China.

Once the Zhou came to power, the duke of Zhou, King Wu's brother, was another important leader. He

was respected for following the Zhou tradition of passing the kingship from father to son. When his brother Wu died, the duke did not try to seize power. Instead, he ruled in his nephew's name until he was old enough to become king.

The early Zhou rulers and the men who followed them tried to improve conditions in China. The duke of Zhou believed that people with the most skill, not just nobles, should run the government. Wu and Wen were said to have written the *Yi Jing*, or *Book of Changes*, though modern scholars doubt it. This important text was said by some people to predict the future. Others saw it as a source of wisdom for the correct way to act in various situations.

Confucius read the *Yi Jing*. He also knew some of the poems written about Wen and his sons. One of them praised Wen, saying his "power was very bright … and very good." And the duke of Zhou was honored because "he has shown

The Shang was the first known dynasty of China. It dates from about 1570 B.C. Some Chinese claim there were earlier dynasties, but there is no written record of their existence. The Shang left two main sources of written records. First, they carved characters into turtle shells and the bones of cattle. Together these carved items are called oracle bones. An oracle is someone or something that tells the future. The Shang oracles studied cracks that appeared in the bones and shells when they were heated. The size and number of cracks were thought to predict the future. The prediction was then written on the oracle bones. The Shang also left carvings on bronze bowls called vessels.

compassion to us people. He has greatly helped us."
Records show that the duke believed in fair trials for
accused criminals, and he tried to treat his subjects
kindly. But the reality was sometimes different from
the duke's ideal. Nobles still often treated peasants
cruelly, and a saying of the time was, "Punishments
do not extend up to the great officers."

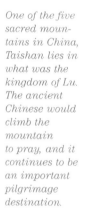

One of the five sacred mountains in China, Taishan lies in what was the kingdom of Lu. The ancient Chinese would climb the mountain to pray, and it continues to be an important pilgrimage destination.

The duke of Zhou's son had ruled Lu centuries before Confucius was born. Many important documents from the dynasty were kept in Lu, so Confucius was able to study them. He believed that the early Zhou leaders had restored the past greatness of ancient China. Their methods, he believed, could help China again as it went through the wars among the various kingdoms and the hardships they created for the peasants. Confucius eventually thought he was the person to spread that old wisdom to China's leaders. ❧

3 INFLUENCES ON A GREAT MIND

During his early 20s, around the time of his mother's death, Confucius added to his duties. In addition to working his low-level government job, he started to teach. But the young scholar did not have a school or classroom he called his own. For many years, he did not even call himself a teacher. To the Chinese of his day, a teacher was someone who had mastered a certain skill, such as painting or making music. Confucius simply saw himself as someone with good ideas on how people should live. One of his students was once asked from whom Confucius had learned. The student said the Master had learned from everyone. Confucius willingly embraced good ideas, no matter where they came from.

Confucius' first students were most likely men

When Confucius is depicted as a teacher, he is nearly always seated.

just slightly younger than he. They met, perhaps, in Confucius' home. Gathered around him, the students listened to Confucius talk about the classic books and share his views on the proper way to live. At times, Confucius responded to his students' questions and then probed the men with his own. His questions

An 18th-century engraving of Confucius shows him in a library, symbolizing his love of books.

made some students struggle to understand him, but Confucius welcomed that. He knew true learning was not easy.

Some sources say that the adult Confucius was tall—over 6 feet (180 centimeters)—and attractive. Yet popular images of him show the teacher with a bump on his head and a mouth filled with large teeth. No matter what he looked like, Confucius impressed others with his learning. His never-ending belief that humans could and should lead better lives was inspiring.

One of his first students was a teenager named Zilu. When they met, one source says, Zilu proudly carried a spear and talked of his hunting skills. At first, he hoped that Confucius' wisdom could help him hunt better. But Zilu soon saw value in the Master's teaching and remained one of his closest disciples for many decades.

As a teacher, Confucius also continued his own learning. In addition to the *Yi Jing* and the *Book of Songs*, he studied historical documents and writings about rituals. Eager to learn about other

The Yi Jing *and the* Book of Songs *are two of the five ancient Chinese writings called the* Five Classics. *Joining them are the* Book of History, *the* Book of Rituals, *and the* Spring and Autumn Annals. *The books contain historical documents, instructions for rituals, and historical writings. Together, these books are considered the first important works of Confucianism. They are also part of a larger group of books called the 13 Classics. These include the* Analects *and the* Mencius.

people and cultures, he interviewed people he met. In 525 B.C., a guest from another kingdom came to Lu. The visitor was in charge of making sacrifices to dead leaders. Confucius talked with the man for hours to learn about the rites and religion of his kingdom. He was curious to see how others lived and perhaps learn something new about proper actions.

Confucius also studied the actions of able government officials living in other kingdoms. Most, like him, were scholars who came from noble families that had fallen on hard times. Together, these men were called the *shi*, or knights, though many of them never rode into battle. The greatest of the government servants in Confucius' time was Zichan. He had his kingdom's laws carved into bronze so all the citizens would know what was and was not allowed. Zichan also helped improve his country's economy. The *Analects* say that Confucius believed Zichan had four of the traits of a superior man:

> *In his conduct of himself, he was humble;
> in serving his superior, he was respectful;
> in nourishing the people, he was kind; in
> ordering the people, he was just.*

The great thinkers of Confucius' day were increasingly focusing on religion and its role in Chinese society. In early days, the Shang had founded their government as a theocracy—the political leaders were also religious leaders. The dynasty was run according to the rules of its faith, which said dead ancestors should be worshipped. Religious ceremonies included sacrifices to the dead. The Zhou carried on many of these religious practices.

By Confucius' day, however, some people were challenging old beliefs about religion. Before, everyone assumed the spirits or Heaven were directly involved in human affairs. As wars and other problems popped up, a few scholars questioned if Heaven took a daily interest in all the actions of humans.

Confucius is featured on a silk painting. Painting on silk dates back to before paper was invented.

No one argued that gods and Heaven didn't exist, but some claimed that perhaps humans couldn't truly understand them or shouldn't expect the spirits to be directly involved in events on Earth.

Confucius loved the rites and ceremonies of the past. He always argued that they should be performed with deep respect. And he believed in the Way of Heaven, a sense that God had a plan for humans, or goals for how they should act. But his disciples said he did not talk about "strange phenomena [such as omens], feats of strength, disorders, or spirits."

His pupil Zilu asked once about serving the spirits, and Confucius said, "Not yet being able to serve other people, how would you be able to serve the spirits?" When Zilu then asked about death, Confucius replied, "Not yet understanding life; how could you understand death?" Confucius wanted all people to focus first on their lives on Earth and their relations with others. To Confucius, religious ideas were not as important as proper behavior.

Confucius sometimes called his teachings on correct behavior the Way of Man, or simply the Way. The Chinese word for "way" is *dao* (also spelled *tao*). It can be an actual path or roadway, or the direction people take in their lives—the choices they make, the ideas they believe in, the way they live. People could follow the Way by living a moral life, not because they would be rewarded after they died, but because it was the right thing to do. Confucius did not look down on others who believed in an afterlife, but he thought people should first focus on their daily actions and their relations with others. Nations, through their leaders, could also follow the Way if they always acted morally. Following the Way brought its own reward and was the highest goal of human life.

Confucius' ideas on the Way could be compared to religious teachings. Many of the world's great religions create codes of behavior—things people should or should not do. But in some cases, the religions teach that believers should follow those codes to make a god happy or achieve a reward after death. Confucius tried to separate the moral teachings from a sense of god. In later centuries, his approach to ethics was called humanism. It focused on the actions of humans and what they could do to improve their lives. ☙

The idea of following the Way appears in several Asian traditions. A religion and philosophy called Daoism was founded by a Chinese man named Laozi. For Daoists, being at peace with nature and oneself was the right path to follow. They also sought to understand nature and Heaven. Daoists wanted to look beyond the human relationships at the center of Confucianism. Another religion, Buddhism, was founded in India during the sixth century B.C. and came to China hundreds of years later. Its greatest thinkers also talked about a path or way that led to a state called enlightenment. Buddhists believe that humans die and are reborn over and over. Finding enlightenment is the only way to break this cycle and find lasting inner peace.

4 TRAVELING AND TEACHING

❦

Sometime around 515 B.C., Confucius left Lu and traveled to Qi, perhaps in support of the duke of Lu. The duke was trying to regain power from the three noble families that ruled Lu: the Ji, the Meng, and the Shu. He sought the help of others in Lu who detested the noble families and their control of the government. When the duke's plans crumbled, he fled north to Qi.

The journey to Qi may have been risky. Bandits sometimes roamed the lands far from a kingdom's capital where the government had few troops. But Confucius and the others traveling with him safely reached Linzi, the capital of Qi.

Soon after he arrived, Confucius heard local musicians play a form of ancient Chinese music called *shao*. He was so impressed with the musicians' skills, the *Analects* says, that he would rather listen to them play than eat. Confucius said, "I had no idea music could achieve such heights!"

While in Qi, Confucius learned about a great thinker named Guan Zhong. In the seventh century B.C., he had worked closely with a previous duke of Qi to improve the country's government. Guan Zhong

A statue of a man playing the qin, a stringed instrument, is more than 2,000 years old.

and the duke set limits on the prices of goods, set standards for weights and measures, and took control of salt and iron production. Their efforts helped the government make more money.

Years later, Confucius told his disciples that Guan Zhong "enabled the duke to become leader of the various feudal lords, uniting and bringing order to the empire. Even today the people still benefit from his largesse [generosity]." Confucius claimed that if Guan Zhong had not advised the duke, Qi and neighboring lands such as Lu would have been overrun by barbarians. Like Confucius, Guan Zhong came from the class of shi. Perhaps his success gave Confucius hope that one day he would also help shape a government.

During the time of Confucius' visit, Duke Jing ruled Qi. The duke asked Confucius about the best way to govern. Confucius replied, "The ruler must rule, the minister [be a] minister, the father [be a] father, and the son [be a] son." Confucius believed that all people had certain roles to play in life, an idea he stressed in his teachings. Their goal was to perform the duties of that role as best they could. The duke thought highly of this answer, and some sources say he offered Confucius a government position. Confucius turned it down, however, saying he had not done anything to deserve the honor of working for the duke.

China in the time of Confucius is sometimes called a feudal society. The word feudalism was first used to describe a system of governing that developed in Europe after 800 A.D. Kings awarded land to nobles, and the nobles promised to be loyal to the kings and provide military services. The nobles were allowed to rule their lands almost as if they were independent states; the king did not tell them how to rule, as long as the nobles remained loyal. Peasants worked the nobles' lands and had little freedom to do as they pleased. This model from Europe loosely fit the way ancient China was governed.

Duke Jing perhaps could have benefited from Confucius' wisdom. The *Analects* report that the duke later died a wealthy man with "a thousand teams of horses." But his riches did not make him a good ruler, because when he died, "the common people felt no sense of gratitude out of which to praise him." In contrast, Confucius taught, men of good character are praised even if they die poor and starving.

Also while in Qi, Confucius seemed to come into conflict with one of the duke's advisers. The adviser thought Confucius did not deserve a job because he was too concerned with ceremonies and too sure of himself. Confucius must have struck some people as arrogant, since he was so confident that his ideas were right. Yet in his personal relationships, he showed compassion for others. One story in the *Analects* says that when a fire burned down a barn, Confucius immediately asked, "Has any man been hurt?" Horses were valuable property, and other people of the day might have been more concerned about them than the peasants who worked in the barn. In contrast, Confucius always stressed humans and their well-being.

Confucius' lessons included poetry, music, and history.

When Confucius finally returned to Lu, he put all his energy into teaching. Instead of casual chats with students, he opened what some historians have called the first private school in China strictly geared to educating the mind. (Records from before Confucius' time show that there were schools for archery, and Confucius also studied this skill.) Some of his first students may have included two sons of the Meng family, one of the three most important families of Lu. The sons supposedly studied ritual with Confucius, since by now he was a known expert on religious and social rites.

But not all of his students came from wealthy and powerful families. Many of them were shi, and many were poor. Confucius took any student who wanted to learn from him, even if all they could offer to pay him was some dried meat. More important than money was the desire to learn and become a better person. Confucius said, "I do not open the way for students who are not driven with eagerness."

Some sources say that Confucius had as many as 3,000 students, though modern historians doubt this. The *Analects* mention just 22 by name, and Mencius claimed that about 70 men studied with the Master. Confucius' school was most likely not like today's schools. None of his students took tests, and he probably met with only a few of them at a time. He talked to them and questioned them about the books

萬世師表

One popular
piece of
art shows
Confucius with
72 scholars in
his temple.

he had them read, including the *Book of Rituals* and the *Book of Songs*. At times, Confucius argued with his students, but he would admit if he made a mistake. Above all, he tried to be honest with his students. "There is nothing I do that I do not share with you," he said. "This is the person I am."

Confucius wanted to prepare young men so they would have the skills to work in government. The students could put Confucius' ideas to work if they served dukes or other officials who ran a kingdom. Confucius' goal was to create the best, fairest governments to help the most people possible. He believed his ideas would make that happen.

But having practical skills was not enough. Confucius also wanted his students to become *junzi*. In English, this means "ruler's son." The term once referred to a member of the ancient Chinese nobility who owned land and might someday rule. To Confucius, however, a junzi was a "gentleman"—someone who always acted morally and followed the teachings on rituals. A person did not need wealth and power to be a gentleman. In fact, the thirst for those things sometimes prevented men from becoming gentlemen.

Gentlemen also studied music

There is no record of Confucius having any female students. The Book of Poetry said that in ancient China, "A woman has nothing to do with public affairs." Women were expected to get married, have children, and take care of the home. Poor women were sometimes sent to work for noble families, to weave and do other chores. Although most women were treated poorly, a noble woman was sometimes educated and could influence her husband's decisions.

Confucius played the qin, an instrument believed to enrich the heart and elevate the human spirit.

and archery. Confucius played a musical instrument and liked to join in when others sang. But skills and knowledge, Confucius said, had no value if a person was not good to others. "If people are not humane [kind], what is the use of rites? If people are not humane, what is the use of music?" With this basic idea, Confucius set out to change China. 𝒮

5 THE MASTER AND HIS STUDENTS

As a teacher, Confucius constantly challenged his students to look carefully at themselves. How they thought and acted shaped what others thought of them. If his students did enter government service, their correct behavior would influence others around them. Confucius asked his disciples, "What has one who is not able to govern himself to do with governing others?" Those who did not behave correctly had no business influencing governments.

Confucius' students included his son, Boyu, whom he did not treat any differently than the others who came to his school. Like the other students, Boyu studied the *Book of Songs* and other classic works. Confucius believed, "If you do not learn the odes [songs], you will not be fit to converse with ... if

Confucius has inspired artists of many nationalities, including Japanese artist Kano Tanyu (1602–1674).

49

you do not learn the rules of propriety, your character cannot be established." Boyu followed his father's orders, but to the Master's disappointment, his son never got a government job.

Several other students did get jobs in government. Zilu worked for the Ji family in Lu and served the Kong family in Wei. Despite this success, Confucius sometimes criticized Zilu for taking action without thinking first. Zilu once asked the Master whom he would want with him if he were in charge of a great army. Perhaps Zilu was hoping Confucius would pick him or someone like him—bold and brave. But Confucius said that a man who "would wrestle a tiger bare-handed" or take some other risky action would not be his choice. Instead, Confucius wanted someone "who would approach any situation with trepidation [caution], and who would be fond of planning with an eye to success." Yet Confucius admired Zilu's loyalty to him, and he once said that his being strict with Zilu was a sign of love for him.

Another of Confucius' most successful students was Zigong. He held several government positions for the Ji family and was known for his skills as a diplomat. Some people even claimed he was equal to Confucius when it came to learning and wisdom. Zigong, however, quickly corrected people with those views. He said, "Confucius is the sun and moon which no one can climb beyond. ... The Master

月百姿
詩書の
月
子路

*Confucius
thought of Zilu
as one of his
closest friends.*

cannot be matched just as a ladder cannot be used to climb the sky."

Confucius had a close relationship with Zilu and Zigong. He seems to have been less close with Ran You, another of his top students. Ran You was more concerned with collecting taxes and rising to positions of power than strictly following the Master's teachings. According to Mencius, Confucius said of Ran You, "He's no follower of mine. If you sounded the drums and attacked him … it wouldn't be such a bad thing." The Master would not mind if people like Ran You were forced out of power.

Of all his students, Confucius loved Yan Hui the best. Yan Hui came from a poor family and remained poor his whole life. Confucius praised the student's attitude; even though he was poor, Yan Hui still enjoyed life.

Confucius considered Yan Hui his most successful student in terms of understanding the Way.

Yan Hui never questioned what Confucius taught, and the teacher once took his silence for stupidity. "But when he has withdrawn," Confucius said, "and I examine what he says and does on his own, it illustrates perfectly what I have been saying. Indeed, there is nothing slow about Yan Hui!" Yan Hui's actions were a perfect model of Confucius' Way.

With these and his other students, Confucius stressed several key ideas. He believed following these ideas would turn his students into gentlemen. The most important trait for a gentleman was *ren*. This word has several translations, but it basically means kindness or love between people. Confucius saw ren as a level of kindness hard for humans to attain, given their many flaws. Yet the goal of life was to come as close to the perfect state of kindness or virtue as possible.

Achieving ren took hard work. A gentleman had to improve himself through education and proper actions. The key to this was *li*, or rituals. The word *propriety* is sometimes used when translating Confucius' teachings on li. Being polite is part of propriety, because it shows respect to others. Propriety was also concerned with following the correct methods of honoring the dead or carrying out other important acts. To become a gentleman, Confucius told his disciples, they had to know what was proper to do on any occasion. He said:

Confucius loved music, and he saw its value in education. Learning to play an instrument required discipline and concentration. Musicians have to follow rules and be able to work with others. The Chinese associated all these qualities with li. Confucius and his followers thought that some music stirred positive thoughts and emotions in listeners, while others produced negative emotions. The ancient Chinese played several stringed instruments, bells, and drums. Archaeologists have also found wind instruments in China that date back before Confucius' time. The xuan was similar to the modern ocarina, a small, rounded flute. The ancient Chinese version had one hole for the mouth and five or so finger holes.

Look not at what is contrary to propriety; listen not to what is contrary to propriety; speak not what is contrary to propriety; make no movement which is contrary to propriety.

Another key part of Confucius' teaching was *yi*. This is sometimes translated as "justice" or "what is right." For Confucius, the right thing to do could depend on the situation. A person had to consider if a correct action in one situation might cause harm in another. The gentleman always relied on his sense of yi, ren, and li to make the right decision and take the right action. Confucius thought people should try to make money and live comfortably, if they could. But how they made their money should not harm others. He said that "wealth and position gained through inappropriate [incorrect] means" were as distant to him as the clouds. A person should always try to do what is right while earning a living or exercising political power.

在陳絕糧
楚使人聘孔子于故陳蔡大夫謀曰
孔子賢而所刺皆中諸侯之疾國
之短集然為政其聘孔子經不來
於是吳楚絕陳蔡子路恩孔子甚慍

Confucius welcomed men of all social classes to study with him.

To Confucius, doing the right thing at all times was part of the Way set down by Heaven. He believed that people should not follow the Way because they feared angering spirits or a god. They should follow it because it was simply the right thing to do. Following correct behavior was important for creating the best society possible.

Confucius' teachings helped people improve themselves and their relations with others. The most important relations, Confucius said, were with family members. In this, he followed ancient Chinese beliefs. Since ancient times, long before Confucius, the Chinese had put the family at the center of human life. The family included several generations with aunts, uncles, and cousins, though only the wealthiest people could afford to have all their relatives live in one house. The father was the head of the family. He made rules for his wife and children and punished them when they disobeyed. Still, adult children and other relatives could have a say in important family decisions.

Children were expected to show honor and obedience to their parents, which is called filial piety.

The theme of filial piety is shown in a 17th-century wall painting. A son protected his father by gaining control over the tiger.

The honoring of dead parents and generations of grandparents led to a form of religion called ancestor worship. Living family members made sacrifices to honor the spirits of those dead relatives. In some cases, the living hoped that by making these sacrifices, the dead would give them aid or advice.

Confucius believed strongly in filial piety and that parents should be shown respect even after they died. He showed this when he mourned his mother for three years. He often spoke about the duties of children to their parents. He said giving elderly parents food and shelter was not enough; "even dogs and horses are given that much care." Showing respect through gentlemanlike behavior was the most important duty. Parents should never have to worry that their children might behave badly. "Give your mother and father nothing to worry about beyond your physical well-being," Confucius said.

Many ancient peoples shared a common bit of advice. This saying is sometimes called the Golden Rule. Confucius shared several versions of this saying with his students. "What you do not want done to yourself, do not do to others." A common version of the phrase is "Do unto others as you would have others do unto you." Ancient Greek philosophers offered up similar advice around 100 years earlier. And 500 years after Confucius lived, Jesus is quoted in the Bible giving his disciples similar advice. Another 600 years after that, the Muslim prophet Muhammad told his followers, "Hurt no one so that no one may hurt you." In fact, almost every major religion in the world today has a saying similar to the Golden Rule.

Modern Chinese families continue to feel a deep respect and sense of responsibility for one another.

Loyalty to relatives extended to matters of law. A duke told Confucius that in his land, a son told on his father when the father stole a sheep. Confucius believed that parents and children should not tell on each other, even if they commit a crime. The bond of family should be stronger than legal matters.

Modern scholars believe that Confucius saw a link between the family and the nation. The filial piety learned within the family served as a model for behavior outside of it. By obeying parents and sharing with relatives, children learned values that would make them good citizens or rulers. Although Confucius wanted to serve in government, he believed people could help the government simply by treating each other well. He quoted the *Book of Documents*:

> *"Just being filial to your parents and befriending your brothers is carrying out the work of government." In doing this I am employed in governing.*

Confucius believed that the act of learning made someone a better person. But learning was not enough by itself. "Having studied, to then repeatedly apply what you have learned—is this not a source of pleasure?" Students must apply what they have learned to get the most benefit from their lessons.

But perhaps even more important than knowledge was wisdom. Confucius gave his disciple Zilu his definition of wisdom: "To know what you know and what you do not know—this then is wisdom." ॐ

6 PUBLIC OFFICIAL

❦

Although Confucius had great success as a teacher, he still hoped to receive a government position as a top minister to the rulers of Qi. He knew that some people questioned his talents. A villager from Daxiang said Confucius was "broad in his learning, and yet he is not renowned [famous] in any particular area." When the comment got back to him, Confucius tried to joke about it. "What should I specialize in? Perhaps charioteering? Or maybe archery? No, I think I'll take charioteering." But Confucius must have felt slightly disappointed, knowing that his students could get government jobs and he could not.

The chance to take a government job finally came around 501 B.C. Members of the Ji family struggled with each other to control Lu. A man named Yang

Huo used this time of trouble to seize power. Like Confucius, Yang Huo was a member of the shi. For about four years, he ruled as a tyrant in Lu. Around 502, he plotted to kill Ji Huanzi, the head of the Ji family. His efforts sparked a civil war. Forces loyal to the Ji forced Yang Huo from power, and he fled to the kingdom of Qi.

At some point, Yang Huo offered Confucius his first major government job. Confucius, however, did not want to work for Yang Huo. He did not approve of the way the tyrant seized power illegally. Yang Huo would not give up. He finally sent Confucius a pig as a gift, hoping to force Confucius to come to see him and thank him. He knew that Confucius' sense of ritual and honor would lead the Master to acknowledge the gift. Yet Confucius still wanted nothing to do with Yang Huo. He waited until he knew the ruler was out before going to his home and thanking him. By chance, the two men met on the road.

"Come with me!" Yang Huo said. "Can you call someone wise who has always wanted to serve in office but who repeatedly misses the opportunity to do so?" The *Analects* says that Confucius replied, "All right, all right, I will serve in office then." Historians now suggest that he did not work for Yang Huo because he did not respect him or how he governed.

Another chance to serve in office soon followed. This time, the offer came from Gongshan Furao, who also served the Ji family of Lu and had command of the walled city of Bi. Gongshan Furao also wanted to rebel against the Ji. Unlike Yang Huo, however, he did not want power just for himself. He wanted to give some control back to the duke of Lu.

Confucius still felt loyal to the duke, so he was tempted by the offer. His student, Zilu, however, convinced him not to take the job. Zilu by this time was working for the Ji family and didn't want Gongshan Furao to have Confucius' help. But he also thought the Master should not associate with a rebel. Confucius took Zilu's advice. Still, he imagined what he could have done, saying he could have helped Gongshan Furao create a great empire.

At the age of 50, Confucius finally got his chance to serve the Ji family. Even though he had been loyal

Ji Kangzi took over from his father as the ruler of Lu in 492 B.C. and ruled until 469. He is mentioned more often in the Analects *than any other person who was not a follower of Confucius. Ji Kangzi asked the teacher how to make the people respectful and eager to do what they should. Confucius replied, "Raise up those who are adept [skilled] and instruct those who are not and the people will be eager." Another time Confucius told Ji Kangzi the best way to govern: "Governing effectively is doing what is proper. If you, sir, lead by doing what is proper, who would dare do otherwise?"*

to the duke of Lu in the past, the Ji were now the accepted rulers. Confucius did not think he was going against his moral code by working for them. Zilu might have used his influence with the Ji to get him the job. Confucius was also friendly with Ji Kangzi, the son of Ji Huanzi.

Ancient sources say that Confucius held several important positions while working for the Ji family. Mencius and several other writers claim he served as the minister of justice who was in charge of all the courts. Modern historians, however, doubt this claim. They argue that such an important job would have been given to a noble. Confucius might have served under the minister of justice. Some sources say he was also a magistrate in the town of Zhongdu and an assistant minister of public works. In Chinese kingdoms, this government department oversaw such projects as digging canals and building dams. However, no one knows what Confucius' duties were as assistant minister.

There is no record that Confucius ever advised

A 20th-century illustration depicted Confucius in a powerful role.

the leader, Ji Huanzi, but he did meet several times with Duke Ding of Lu. Although the Ji held the true power in the kingdom, the duke still played a part in the government. He asked Confucius, "Is there any one saying that can make a state prosper?" Confucius replied no, but he added that it was important for a ruler to understand the difficulty of ruling.

The duke then asked if any one saying can ruin a state. Again Confucius said no. He added that a state could be ruined if a ruler said useless things and no one questioned him.

Confucius saw problems with Lu's government. The kingdom was no longer following the Way. Power had moved from the duke, where it rightfully

Confucius is depicted wearing an imperial crown, which was worn only by emperors and the Jade Emperor, the supreme ruler of Heaven.

belonged, to the Ji and the other ruling families. These families did not have Heaven's support to rule. And within the families, the leaders were not making sure their decisions were followed. Government orders were being carried out by advisers and the people who ran their households. The leaders were too far from the center of power, Confucius believed, for the government to succeed. He said, "It is unlikely the state will survive beyond three generations."

Although there is little record of what Confucius did while serving the Ji, the *Analects* do record some of his behavior and appearance at that time. When speaking to officials with less power than he held, Confucius was friendly. "And when speaking with higher officials," the *Analects* say, he was "straightforward yet respectful. In the presence of his lord [ruler], he was reverent [respectful] though composed [calm]."

As a master of ritual and proper

One of the most exciting tales told about Confucius' time in government may have never happened. Sometime around 499 B.C., the sources say, he went with the duke of Lu on an official visit to Qi. The legend says Confucius prevented the leaders of Qi from kidnapping the duke. Then he convinced Qi to give back lands it had taken from Lu. Some modern historians accept that Confucius did make this journey, but they reject the heroic tale. In the years after Confucius died, some of his disciples felt a need to make up stories that made Confucius seem more important than he really was. They thought building up his image as a great man would convince more people to follow his teachings.

behavior, Confucius always knew how to act around important guests. "He would salute the others standing in attendance, gesturing his clasped hands to the right and to the left." As the other ministers of the day did, he wore long flowing robes while on official business. He walked with grace and energy, and he always seemed sure of himself.

The *Analects* also record how Confucius lived his private life. When he ate, he did not talk, and he didn't eat between meals. Before he ate even the simplest meal, he made an offering to the spirits. When he sat, Confucius made sure the mats were lined up just so.

At times, the Chinese took part in rituals that prepared them for offering sacrifices or other religious duties. These acts were called purification. The rituals were supposed to clean the people taking part in religious ceremonies, both inside and out. If they were clean, the gods would look more favorably on their actions. When Confucius took part in purification, he swapped his fancy robes for a simple cloth coat. He also ate less food and slept apart from his wife.

Following all these rules might have made Confucius seem stiff, but he had a sense of humor. Once when he heard some awful music, he joked that it sounded like someone was using a huge ax to kill a chicken. He also enjoyed drinking wine, though he never got drunk.

朝
亡

Confucius highly valued religious ceremonies.

Confucius' life as a minister was not demanding. The Ji seemed to have given him a job out of respect for his teaching skills and to keep him from serving any other noble family. They didn't really want his advice on how to run the government. Being ignored upset Confucius, and he decided to quit his government post. Along with some of his disciples, he left Lu, looking for rulers more willing to take his advice.

7 TRAVELS ABROAD

⤷⤶⤷⤶

As with many parts of Confucius' life, his travels abroad are not well recorded. An ancient Chinese history book gives three different years for when he left Lu. Most likely, it was sometime between 498 and 493 B.C. Historians also don't know how many disciples went with him, but some of his closest, including Zilu and Yan Hui, made the trip. Other disciples might have joined the Master later during his travels.

Confucius and his followers first went to Wei, just west of Lu. They rode in horse-drawn wagons over well-built roads. In Wei, Confucius made contact with several government officials. Zilu's wife had a sister who was married to a noble. This noble told Zilu, "If Confucius will stay at my home, I'll make him a minister here in Wei." Some sources say

During his journeys to various kingdoms, Confucius met with many dukes and other leaders.

Confucius took the position; others say he did not. But he clearly did stay for a time with an official named Yan Chouyou.

In the lands he visited, Confucius received money from the governments. The money was not a salary for a job. Instead, the foreign rulers gave it as a gift to honor Confucius as a wise teacher. Without this help, he and his disciples would have struggled to survive.

On this trip or perhaps another trip to Wei, a disciple noted that the kingdom's population was large. The disciple asked Confucius, "When the people are already so numerous, what more can be done for them?" Confucius replied, "Make them prosperous [wealthy]." After that, Confucius said, the next step was to educate them. Although Confucius cherished the value of education, he knew the people first needed food, clothing, and shelter.

From Wei, Confucius and his followers headed to Chen. On the way, they passed through the

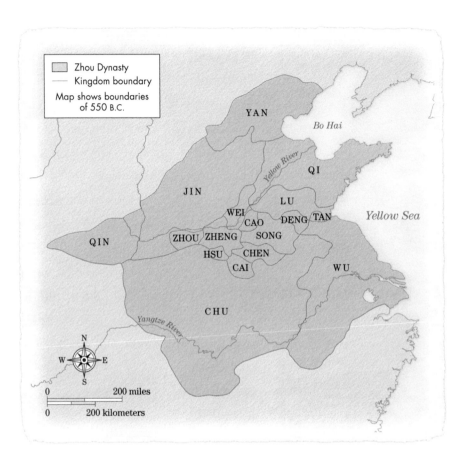

Zhou Dynasty
— Kingdom boundary
Map shows boundaries
of 550 B.C.

YAN

Bo Hai

Yellow River

QI

JIN

LU

WEI
CAO DENG TAN

Yellow Sea

ZHOU ZHENG SONG

QIN

HSU CHEN

CAI

WU

CHU

Yangtze River

0   200 miles

0   200 kilometers

kingdom of Song. For some reason, the minister of
war there, a man named Huan Tui, wanted to kill
Confucius. Huan Tui's brother Sima Niu had studied with the Master, and one historian thinks the
relationship between the brother and Confucius
angered Huan Tui. Like many nobles of the day, the
minister thought his family's background made him
better than others. He used his power to force others
to give him money. Or Huan Tui might have disliked

*To reach Chen
from Wei,
Confucius had
to pass through
Cao and Song.*

73

the ideas Confucius taught his brother and others. Some nobles did not believe they should have to be gentlemen, or that people who were not nobles could be equal to them.

Because of the angry minister, Mencius wrote, the Master "had to travel through Sung [Song] in disguise." He finally reached Chen, where "he stayed with the pure Mayor Chen." During his time in Chen, Confucius met with the minister of justice, and Mencius says he advised the local duke.

Around this time, Confucius also visited a neighboring land of Cai. There he met the duke of Shê, a noble from Chu. Ancient books suggest that the duke accepted some of the ideas Confucius taught. He

Though he was never appointed a chief adviser to any leader, Confucius made an impression on the dukes he met with.

was said to be a moral person who treated others well. At their meeting, the two men discussed the proper way to rule. Confucius said, "Good government obtains [happens] when those who are near are made happy, and those who are far off are attracted." In other words, people outside a land would see how well its citizens were ruled, and they would want to live there, too.

At one point, the duke of Shê asked Zilu what kind of man Confucius was. Zilu did not reply. Confucius later asked his disciple:

Why didn't you just say to him: As a person, Confucius is driven by such eagerness to teach and learn that he forgets to eat, he enjoys himself so much that he forgets to worry, and does not even realize that old age is on its way.

During his stay in Chen, Confucius seems to have gotten another offer to serve in government. At the time, the kingdom of Qin was fighting a civil war. Two groups

The traditional lands of the Zhou Dynasty were centered in the plains of northern China. Far to the south of this, people of different ethnic backgrounds settled and built a huge state known as Chu. Over time, the people of Chu adopted the Zhou culture, though they did not pledge their loyalty to Zhou rulers. The Chu also battled the Zhou states to their north. By the end of the sixth century B.C., Chu had taken over about 50 smaller neighbors. It was the most powerful state in southern China. By the time the Master was born, Chu was battling Wu to dominate southern China. Wu invaded Chu in 506 and almost destroyed the kingdom. Chu managed to survive the attack, but it eventually became part of the larger Qin Empire.

of nobles were battling for control, with their duke caught in the middle. An official from one of the noble families invited Confucius to serve in their city. Confucius considered the offer, but finally said no. At the time, the nobles who sought his help were technically rebels. Confucius thought it would not be proper to work for people challenging the legal government.

For much of the time Confucius traveled, no one recorded what he did or where he went. The *Analects* mention foreigners that he met, but it's not clear if the meetings took place during this time. Finally, in 484, Confucius returned to Wei. He found a kingdom in chaos.

Confucius is said to have traveled by ox cart.

In previous years, the duke's son had plotted to kill his mother. When his plan was discovered, the prince was forced to flee. When the duke died, his grandson, not the prince, took the throne. At the same time, some of the duke's enemies helped the prince return to Wei and try to take power. When Confucius reached Wei, the prince and his son were struggling to control Wei. Meanwhile, a minister named Kong You held the real power. Kong You gave Confucius money and asked for his advice. Although the minister was not a gentleman, as Confucius defined it, he won some praise from the Master. Confucius said that Kong You "was fond of study, not ashamed to ask questions of those below him in rank."

Soon, however, Confucius saw that Kong You was more interested in power than in propriety. When the minister asked Confucius for advice on a military campaign, Confucius refused to help and made plans to leave Wei. At that moment, a message came from Lu. The ruling Ji family wanted him to return to his homeland. Ten years of wandering were about to end. ❧

8 LAST YEARS

❧✦❧

Confucius was nearing 70 years old when he returned to Lu and walked the streets of Qufu that he knew so well. The duke at the time was named Ai, but it was the Master's old friend Ji Kangzi who had invited him to return. Perhaps some of Confucius' former students working for the Ji also played a part in the invitation.

Once again, Confucius seemed to receive a lowly government job, but he had some contact with Duke Ai and the three families that held the real power in Lu. When Ji Kangzi wanted to raise taxes, he sent Confucius' student Ran You to the Master, perhaps to get his approval. Confucius opposed the tax increase, but Ji Kangzi ordered it collected anyway. Ran You, who was in charge of collecting the taxes, obeyed

A 1690 A.D. engraving depicted a tax collector. Some tax collectors were thought to abuse their power, taking more money than the people could afford to give.

Ji Kangzi. As a result, Confucius lost respect for Ran You, one of his best students, for carrying out a policy that hurt the poor people of Lu.

Ji Kangzi was not the only leader to ignore Confucius. At the end of 482 B.C., a duke in Qi was killed by one of his soldiers. Although Qi and Lu had sometimes battled each other, Confucius thought that Lu leaders should try to stop the killer and his supporters from seizing power. These rebels might pose an even greater risk to Lu than the previous duke. Confucius went to Duke Ai and said, "I implore [beg] you to send an army to punish him [the killer]." The duke, however, needed the approval of the Three Families. When Confucius met with them, they refused to send troops to Qi.

Though Confucius' influence in government was limited, he continued to gain pleasure from teaching. He seemed to have found a new group of students eager to learn his ideas. These men did not achieve high government jobs as Zilu and Ran You did. But they became important teachers, helping to spread the Master's ideas. One of the most important was Zengzi, or Master Zeng, who stressed the importance of filial piety. He is mentioned several times in the *Analects*.

Zengzi
(505–c.436 B.C.)

During these later years in Lu, Confucius also turned his attention to the ancient texts he had studied for so long. He said that after he returned from Wei, "I revised the *Book of Poetry*, and put the 'Songs of the Kingdom' and the 'Ceremonial Hymns'

Confucius' grand-
son Zisi played an
important role in
spreading the ideas
of Confucianism. He
was too young to study
with his grandfather,
but he must have
learned from one or
more of his students.
Zisi went on to become
a teacher himself. His
students supposedly
included the man who
taught Confucianism
to Mencius. Zisi is
credited with writing
some, if not most, of
the Doctrine of the
Mean, a book that
expanded on some of
the Master's teachings.
In 1993, archaeologists
found new examples of
Zisi's work in Guodian,
China. Other students
of Confucianism also
worked with Zisi on
these writings. Modern
scholars say that these
writings talked more
about human emotions
than Confucius did in
the Analects.

in proper order." The *Historical Records* suggests that Confucius took 3,000 poems and chose 305 to go into his new version of the *Book of Poetry*. Modern historians, however, are not sure that he did more than change the order of the poems in the book.

Confucius was also given credit for editing the *Spring and Autumn Annals*, documents about the history of Lu. Mencius quoted him as saying, "If people understand me, it's because of the *Spring and Autumn Annals*; and if they condemn me, it's also because of the *Spring and Autumn Annals*." Historians now think that Confucius did not edit the book.

After his return to Lu, Confucius mourned the loss of several people close to him. The first to die was Boyu, his only son. He died shortly after giving Confucius a grandson who was later known as Zisi. When Boyu died, Confucius refused to honor him with a fancy funeral. He believed that a simple coffin and ceremony were enough for any person.

Yan Hui was the next person to die who was dear to Confucius. The death of this beloved disciple upset the Master tremendously. "Heaven is the ruin of me," he cried, "Heaven is the ruin of me!" His disciples worried that Confucius' grief was too much. Confucius said, "If I don't grieve with abandon for him, then for whom?" The Master said that Yan Hui, out of all his students, was the one who loved learning the most. He felt as close to Yan Hui as his own son—and perhaps even closer.

The Temple of Yan Hui, named in honor of the favorite disciple, stands in Qufu.

Two more disciples soon died. One was Sima Niu, the brother of Huan Tui, the man who had wanted to kill Confucius during his trip through Song. The

Confucius was buried in Qufu in a wooded setting near his son, Boyu. In the centuries since, many of his descendants have been buried nearby. Emperors of China donated land to the family, creating a graveyard that covers about 81 acres (32.4 hectares). Today the Kong family cemetery, called Confucius Forest, features statues of the Master. In 1961, the cemetery was named one of 180 sites protected by the Chinese government. It is near a temple built to honor Confucius and a home owned by his descendants. Through the centuries, some of China's emperors made improvements to the building. The temple, family home, and cemetery are popular tourist attractions.

next year, in 480, Zilu died. Of all the disciples, Zilu was perhaps the closest in age to Confucius, and they had known each other for more than 40 years. Confucius had once predicted, "He will not die a natural death." The Master knew that Zilu's bold ways would get him into trouble. In the end, Confucius was right. Zilu had gone to Wei to serve a noble family there. When a rebellion broke out in Wei shortly after his arrival, Zilu refused to flee. He was killed trying to protect his lord.

Less than a year later, Confucius himself was dead. No one knows how he died. A report in a historical document merely says, "Summer, a day in the fourth month, Confucius died." Mencius reports that his disciples mourned him for three years, just as Confucius had said children should do for their parents. Zigong, one of the older students, had been close to Confucius during his last years. He mourned the Master for an additional three years. Another

disciple who honored Confucius was You Juo. He was so respected that he was called Master You. He said, "From the birth of mankind until now, there has never been the equal of Confucius."

A stone burial mound was erected at Confucius' tomb in 1443.

9 THE TRIUMPH OF CONFUCIANISM

During his lifetime, Confucius never achieved his goal of winning a high government position. But his teachings and personal behavior had influenced his students. Even some leaders saw the importance of his life and ideas. Just two years after the Master died, Duke Gun of Lu honored him. He had Confucius' home in Qufu turned into a temple, where his books, musical instruments, and other prized items were kept.

In the centuries that followed, the Master's former students helped shape what is now called Confucianism. They taught others using Confucius' methods, and these students then became teachers themselves.

Confucius was one of many intelligent men who developed ideas about government and society

Confucius' influence on China and surrounding countries lives on, nearly 2,500 years after his death.

Mozi was born around 470 B.C., just about the time Confucius died. Scholars know even less about his life than they do about the Master's. Like Confucius, Mozi thought skilled men, not just nobles, should be allowed to hold key public offices. Unlike Confucius, Mozi did not see much value in music and ritual, or in people trying to find virtue in their lives. He believed in strict obedience to government rulers, saying, "What the superior thinks to be right, all must think to be right; what the superior thinks to be wrong, all must think to be wrong." Mozi also believed everyone should love each other completely. He said, "Partial love is the cause of all the human calamities [problems] in the world. Partial love is wrong without fail."

during the Spring and Autumn Period. The era is sometimes called the Hundred Schools of Thought. Confucianism, along with Daoism, was one of the major schools of thought at that time. Two others were Legalism and Moism. Confucian teachers competed with followers of these other major schools of thought to win new students.

The first Legalist was Xunzi, who was influenced by Confucius. He rejected, however, the notion put forth by Mencius that people were basically good. Xunzi said people were by nature bad, and so they needed a strong government to limit their actions. He believed the government should direct citizens' behaviors. Later Legalists said the people did not even need to be educated. Instead, they should rely on their all-powerful leader to tell them what to do.

Moism came from the teachings of Mozi. He did not agree with Confucius' teaching to study the past for guidance in governing in the present. Instead of following tradition, rulers should do anything possible to create order and help their kingdoms grow. Moism died out by the third century B.C., but Legalism survived, and for a time, it was the official philosophy of a unified China.

In 221 B.C., the ruler of Qin united the kingdoms of China into one vast empire. He was called the First Emperor of Qin (Qin shi huangdi) and the first to govern the whole of China as one empire. He and other

During his rule, Qin shi huangdi outlawed Confucianism and punished its followers.

For some people, "Confucius" might be just a name found in fortune cookies at Chinese restaurants. For years, some of the fortunes started with the words "Confucius say," followed by the fortune. Some jokes have also used the phrase, followed by words clearly not part of the Master's teachings. Today the Chinese government is taking a more serious approach to educating the world about Confucius. It is spending $10 billion on schools called Confucius Institutes. The first have appeared in Canada, South Korea, the United States, Germany, and Kenya. The schools' main goal is to teach the Chinese language and culture to foreigners. At the same time, students learn about Confucius and his role.

Qin nobles followed Legalist teachings. Within 20 years, however, the Qin Dynasty crumbled, and the Han rose to power. Under their rule, government leaders and scholars began to follow Confucianism. The first Han emperor turned to the Confucians because they knew so much about the classic books and rituals. They soon taught the princes of the empire, stressing the importance of treating the common people well. Over time, the leaders also embraced some elements of Daoism and Legalism. But after 136 B.C., they officially hailed Confucianism as China's state philosophy. Soon many people were making sacrifices in Confucius' name, treating him as if he were a god.

The Confucian system of China stressed the need to have educated officials running the government. Men eager to serve had to take tests to prove their skills. Their knowledge, not the power of their families, determined whether they got jobs. Confucius' ideas on

Laozi (center) is called the father of Daoism.

propriety also had great influence.

Over the centuries, Chinese scholars continued to study Confucius' ideas and add to them. At times,

三
聖
圖

The three spiritual leaders, Confucius, Buddha, and Laozi, are often pictured together.

other philosophies became popular and weakened the Confucian influence. Daoism became strong during the third century A.D., and Buddhism emerged several centuries later. At times, elements of Daoism, Buddhism, and Confucianism were blended together. But the Confucian system of education and government service became stronger over time and remained in place until the 20th century. Through China's military conquests, the teachings of Confucius also became important in Korea, Japan, Singapore, and Vietnam.

The decline of Confucianism in China started in 1905. The government ended the system of exams used to find the best government officials. For a time, Confucius was still considered a great teacher. But a new group of leaders was emerging who wanted China to follow modern political systems. Some wanted a democracy as practiced in the United States and parts of Europe. Others supported communism, which called for the government to own all the property. A single political party, the Communist Party, would control the government.

Mao Zedong (1893–1976)

In 1949, communists led by Mao Zedong took over mainland China. Mao had once said, "I hated Confucius from the age of eight." He and others believed Confucian teachings forced the peasants to accept the rule of powerful men. The communists wanted to give power to these people through their party. The communists ended religious practices tied to honoring Confucius. But over time, they accepted his position as a great scholar.

Confucian influence also remained strong on the island of Taipei. Chinese called Nationalists, who opposed the communists, fled there when Mao and his supporters came to power. On Taipei, the Nationalists created the Republic of China, which is also called Taiwan.

Among China's growing cities is Shanghai, with a population of more than 18 million.

With a population of 1.3 billion people, communist China is becoming a powerful, modern nation. More people are leaving farms to work in cities. Some

Chinese are building great fortunes. These changes have shaken traditional ways of life for many Chinese. As China moves forward, it looks to the past—and the teachings of Confucius. In 2005, Chinese president Hu Jintao remarked, "Confucius said, 'Harmony is something to be cherished.'" Some scholars and government leaders think Confucian ideas can bring order as the country faces its changes.

Statues of Confucius are found around the world, showing the scope of his influence.

Confucius would probably be amazed at China today. It covers more land than the kingdoms of his lifetime did, and millions of average people live in a comfort he never could have imagined. But modern life has also weakened tradition and propriety. He would probably approve of the return to some of his old teachings, which have shaped China for more than 2,100 years. ✺

CONFUCIUS' LIFE

551 B.C.

Born in Zou,
Lu (Shandong
Province, China)

c. 548 B.C.

Shuliang He,
Confucius'
father, dies

536 B.C.

Decides to dedicate
his life to learning

550 B.C.

550 B.C.

Cyrus the Great
conquers Media
and founds the
Persian Empire

548 B.C.

First known reference
to Go, an ancient
board game

535 B.C.

The first Roman
calendar is introduced
it has 10 months and
begins in March

WORLD EVENTS

C. **528** B.C.

Mourns for his
mother for three years
following her death;
begins to teach

525 B.C.

Meets with a
foreign guest
and learns about
the country's
religious rites

532 B.C.

Marries and
takes a low-level
government job

530 B.C.

530 B.C.

Temple of Apollo is
built at Corinth

525 B.C.

Greek song and dance
performances evolve
into the first plays

CONFUCIUS' LIFE

C. 517 B.C.

Leaves Lu and stays in Qi; upon his return, opens China's first private school

501 B.C.

Is offered a government position with the Ji family of Lu

C. 499 B.C.

Goes with the duke of Lu on an official visit to Qi

515 B.C.

515 B.C.

Construction of the second Temple in Jerusalem is completed

C. 500 B.C.

Polynesian culture develops in Fiji, Samoa, and Tonga

498 B.C.

Macedonia regains its independence from Persia; Alexander I of Macedonia becomes king

WORLD EVENTS

C. 495 B.C.

Gives up his government job and begins traveling through neighboring kingdoms

484 B.C.

While in Wei, receives an invitation to return to Lu

483 B.C.

Zisi, his grandson, is born

490 B.C.

496 B.C.

Sophocles, Athenian dramatist and statesman, is born

481 B.C.

The Spring and Autumn Period in China ends; the Warring States Period lasts until 256 B.C.

CONFUCIUS' LIFE

479 B.C.

Dies in Qufu, Lu
(Shandong
Province, China)

477 B.C.

Duke Gong of Lu
turns his home
into a temple

480 B.C.

Zilu, his first
student, dies

480 B.C.

480 B.C.

Persians, led by
Xerxes I, invade
Greece; they are later
defeated at the naval
battle of Salamis

470 B.C.

Greek philosopher
Socrates is born

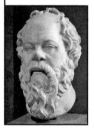

WORLD EVENTS

136 B.C.

Confucianism becomes the official philosophy of China

221 B.C.

The Qin unite the various Chinese kingdoms into one empire

220 B.C.

224 B.C.

Earthquake destroys the Colossus of Rhodes

149 B.C.

Romans annex Macedonia as a province

DATE OF BIRTH: 551 B.C.

BIRTH NAME: Kong Qiu

BIRTHPLACE: Zou, Lu (Shandong Province, China)

FATHER: Shuliang He

MOTHER: Zhengzai

EDUCATION: Various unknown teachers

SPOUSE: Name is unknown

CHILDREN: Boyu (?–483 B.C.) One or perhaps two daughters, names and dates unknown

DATE OF DEATH: 479 B.C.

PLACE OF BURIAL: Qufu, Lu (Shandong Province, China)

Further Reading

Ball, Jacqueline. *Ancient China*. Washington, D.C.: National Geographic, 2007.

Daoism. Peterborough, N.H.: Cobblestone Publishing, 2000.

Freedman, Russell. *Confucius: The Golden Rule*. New York: Arthur A. Levine Books, 2002.

Hoobler, Thomas, and Dorothy Hoobler. *Confucianism*. New York: Facts on File, 2004.

Kleeman, Terry F. *The Ancient Chinese World*. New York: Oxford University Press, 2005.

Slavicek, Louise Chipley. *Confucianism*. San Diego: Lucent Books, 2002.

Tracy, Kathleen. *The Life and Times of Confucius*. Hockessin, Del.: Mitchell Lane Publishers, 2005.

Look for more Signature Lives books about this era:

Alexander the Great: *World Conqueror*

Aristotle: *Philosopher, Teacher, and Scientist*

Hatshepsut: *Egypt's First Female Pharaoh*

Hypatia: *Mathematician, Inventor, and Philosopher*

Julius Caesar: *Roman General and Statesman*

Ramses II: *Egyptian Pharaoh, Warrior, and Builder*

Socrates: *Ancient Greek in Search of Truth*

Thucydides: *Ancient Greek Historian*

On the Web

For more information on this topic, use FactHound.

1. Go to *www.facthound.com*
2. Type in this book ID: 0756538327
3. Click on the *Fetch It* button.

FactHound will find the best Web sites for you.

Historic Sites

Indianapolis Museum of Art
4000 Michigan Road
Indianapolis, IN 46208-3326
317/920-2660
One of the best exhibits of Asian art in the United States

Freer Gallery of Art/
Arthur M. Sackler Gallery
Smithsonian Institution
1050 Independence Ave. S.W.
Washington, D.C. 20013-7012
Large collection of bronze art from ancient China

barbarians
foreign people thought to lack basic learning or manners

democracy
form of government in which the people elect their leaders

descendants
all the relatives who trace their family roots back to
one person

disciples
devoted followers of a religious or moral teacher

dynasty
succession of rulers from the same family; powerful
family or group of people whose members retain their
power and influence through several generations

generation
any group of people born at approximately the same time

magistrate
local government official who often serves as both
lawmaker and judge

minister
high-ranking official in a country's government who
advises the leader

philosophy
system of thought or action based on certain core beliefs

propriety
correct actions and attitudes

sacrifice
offer gifts, particularly dead animals, to honor a god
or spirit

subjects
people ruled by a king or other noble

Chapter 1:
Page 10, line 2: James Legge (trans.). *The Teachings of Confucius*. El Paso, Texas: El Paso Norte Press, 2005, p. 74.
Page 12, line 3: H.G. Creel. *Confucius and the Chinese Way*. New York: Harper Torchbooks, 1949, p. 41.

Chapter 2:
Page 17, line 5: Roger T. Ames and Henry Rosemont Jr. (trans.). *The Analects of Confucius: A Philosophical Translation*. New York: Ballantine Books, 1998, p. 127.
Page 20, line 13: Ibid., p. 206.
Page 20, line 26: Ibid., p. 76.
Page 21, line 5: David Hinton (trans.). *Mencius*. Washington, D.C.: Counterpoint, 1998, p. 187.
Page 23, line 15: Jonathan Clements. *Confucius: A Biography*. Stroud, England: Sutton Publishing, 2004, p. 17.
Page 24, line 3: *The Analects of Confucius*, p. 209.
Page 27, line 26: Howard D. Smith. *Confucius*. New York: Charles Scribner's Sons, 1973, p. 29.
Page 28, line 6: Edwin O. Reischauer and John K. Fairbanks. *East Asia: The Great Tradition*. Boston: Houghton Mifflin Company, 1958, p. 51.

Chapter 3:
Page 34, line 20: *The Teachings of Confucius*, p. 25.
Page 36, line 10: *Confucius and the Chinese Way*, p. 115.
Page 36, line 13: *The Analects of Confucius*, p. 144.

Chapter 4:
Page 40, line 2: Ibid., p. 114.
Page 41, line 6: Ibid., p. 176.
Page 41, line 18: Ibid., p. 156.
Page 42, line 4: Ibid., p. 200.
Page 42, line 27: Ibid., p. 55.
Page 44, line 19: Ibid., p. 112.
Page 46, line 2: Ibid., p. 116.
Page 46, sidebar: H.G. Creel. *The Birth of China*. New York: Frederick Ungar Publishing, 1937, p. 285.
Page 47, line 4: Thomas Cleary (trans.). *The Essential Confucius*. Edison, N.J.: Castle Books, 1998, p. 133.

Chapter 5:
Page 49, line 6: *Confucius and the Chinese Way*, p. 76.
Page 49, line 14: *The Teachings of Confucius*, pp. 99–100.
Page 50, line 13: *The Analects of Confucius*, p. 113.
Page 50, line 27: Ibid., pp. 224–225.
Page 52, line 3: *Mencius*, p. 132.
Page 53, line 3: *The Analects of Confucius*, p. 78.
Page 54, line 1: Ibid., p. 65.

Page 54, line 22: *The Analects of Confucius*, p. 113.

Page 57, line 19: Ibid., p. 77.

Page 57, sidebar: *The Teachings of Confucius*, p. 91.

Page 57, sidebar: "The Last Sermon of the Prophet Muhammad." Islam for Today. 16 April 2008. www.islamfortoday.com/lastsermon.htm

Page 59, line 7: Ibid., pp. 80–81.

Page 59, line 13: *The Analects of Confucius*, p. 71.

Page 59, line 19: Ibid., p. 79.

Chapter 6:

Page 61, line 5: Ibid., p. 126.

Page 62, line 20: Ibid., p. 202.

Page 64, sidebar: Ibid., p. 80.

Page 64, sidebar: Ibid., p. 157.

Page 65, line 4: Ibid., p. 166.

Page 67, line 12: Ibid., p. 196.

Page 67, line 22: Ibid., p. 134.

Page 68, line 2: Ibid.

Chapter 7:

Page 71, line 14: *Mencius*, p. 173.

Page 72, line 17: *The Analects of Confucius*, p. 164.

Page 74, line 6: *Mencius*, pp. 173–174.

Page 75, line 4: *The Teachings of Confucius*, p. 76.

Page 75, line 16: *The Analects of Confucius*, p. 115.

Page 77, line 13: *Confucius and the Chinese Way*, p. 50.

Chapter 8:

Page 81, line 2: *The Analects of Confucius*, p. 177.

Page 81, line 25: Ibid., p. 130.

Page 82, line 13: *Mencius*, p. 113.

Page 83, line 4: *The Analects of Confucius*, pp. 143–144.

Page 84, line 6: *The Teachings of Confucius*, p. 60.

Page 84, line 19: *Confucius*, p. 54.

Page 85, line 3: *Confucius and the Chinese Way*, p. 56.

Chapter 9:

Page 88, sidebar: Ibid., p. 184.

Page 88, sidebar: Richard Hooker. "Chinese Philosophy: Mo Tzu." Washington State University. World Civilizations: An Internet Classroom and Anthology. 1996. 17 Feb. 2007. www.wsu.edu/~dee/CHPHIL/MOTZU.HTM

Page 93, line 20: *Confucius*, p. 193.

Page 95, line 11: Benjamin Robertson and Melinda Liu. "Can the Sage Save China?" *Newsweek International*. 20 March 2006. MSNBC.com. www.msnbc.msn.com/id/11788162/site/newsweek/

Ames, Roger T., and Henry Rosemont Jr. (trans.). *The Analects of Confucius: A Philosophical Translation*. New York: Ballantine Books, 1998.

Chang Chung-yuan. *Tao: A New Way of Thinking*. New York: Perennial Library, 1975.

Chin, Annping. *The Authentic Confucius*. New York: Scribner, 2007.

Cleary, Thomas (trans.). *The Essential Confucius*. Edison, N.J.: Castle Books, 1998.

Clements, Jonathan. *Confucius: A Biography*. Stroud, England: Sutton Publishing, 2004.

"Confucius Forest." ChinaCulture.org. 2003. 16 April 2008. www.chinaculture.org/gb/en_travel/2003-09/24/content_35089.htm

Creel, H.G. *The Birth of China*. New York: Frederick Ungar Publishing, 1937.

Creel, H.G. *Confucius and the Chinese Way*. New York: Harper Torchbooks, 1949.

Hinton, David (trans.). *Mencius*. Washington, D.C.: Counterpoint, 1998.

Hooker, Richard. "Chinese Philosophy." Washington State University. World Civilizations: An Internet Classroom and Anthology. 1996. 16 April 2008. www.wsu.edu/~dee/CHPHIL/CHPHIL.HTM

Legge, James (trans.). *The Teachings of Confucius*. El Paso, Texas: El Paso Norte Press, 2005.

Loewe, Michael, and Edward L. Shaughnessy, eds. *The Cambridge History of Ancient China: From the Origins of Civilization to 221 B.C.* Cambridge, England: Cambridge University Press, 1999.

McIntyre, Stephen R. "The Works of Mencius." nothingistic.org. 2003. 16 April 2008. http://nothingistic.org/library/mencius/toc.html

O'Brien, Patrick (ed.). *Atlas of World History*. New York: Oxford University, 1999.

Reischauer, Edwin O., and John K. Fairbanks. *East Asia: The Great Tradition*. Boston: Houghton Mifflin Company, 1958.

Riegel, Jeffrey. "Confucius." *The Stanford Encyclopedia of Philosophy* (Fall 2006 Edition). 5 Sept. 2006. 14 April 2008. http://plato.stanford.edu/archives/fall2006/entries/confucius/

Robertson, Benjamin, and Melinda Liu. "Can the Sage Save China?" *Newsweek International*. MSNBC.com. 20 March, 2006. 19 Dec. 2007. www.msnbc.msn.com/id/11788162/site/newsweek/

Shen, Andrea. "Ancient Script Rewrites History." *Harvard University Gazette*. 22 Feb. 2001. www.news.Harvard.edu/gazette/2001/02.22/07-ancientscript.html

Smith, D. Howard. *Confucius*. New York: Charles Scribner's Sons, 1973.

"The Temple of Confucius." World Heritage List. October 1994. 16 April 2008. http://whc.unesco.org/archive/advisory_body_evaluation/704.pdf

Michael Burgan is a freelance writer of books for children and adults. A history graduate of the University of Connecticut, he has written more than 100 fiction and nonfiction children's books. For adult audiences, he has written news articles, essays, and plays. Burgan is a recipient of an Educational Press Association of America award.

Image Credits